The author and illustrator would like
to thank everyone in Addenbrooke's
Hospital, Cambridge, for their
enormous help and co-operation in
preparing this book.

This edition first published 2000 by Happy Cat Books,
Bradfield, Essex CO11 2UT

Text copyright © 1973, 1986, 2000 Althea Braithwaite
Illustrations copyright © 2000 Edmund Bright

The moral rights of the author and of the illustrator
have been asserted.

A CIP catalogue record for this book is available from
the British Library

ISBN 1 899248 49 8 Paperback
ISBN 1 899248 44 7 Hardback

Printed in Hong Kong by Wing King Tong Co. Ltd

TALKING IT THROUGH

HOSPITAL

Althea

Illustrated by Edmund Bright

Happy Cat Books

If you have an accident, or if you have not been well for a while, your doctor may send you to hospital to see another doctor or to have some tests.

Doctors, nurses and all the other people working in the hospital are friendly and want to make you feel at home. But it can seem strange and confusing. There are lots of signs telling you where to go and long passages. They are like busy streets with people hurrying past.

Alex couldn't always hear what people said. He had come to hospital to do some tests to see how well his ears worked. When he and his mum found the right clinic, the nurses were very friendly and there were toys to play with.

The tests were more like games. Alex had to listen very carefully and put animals and bricks in baskets when he heard sounds through different machines. His ears were very blocked up, so he couldn't hear all the noises. The doctor says he needs a small operation, to put grommets in his ears. "You will only have to stay in hospital for a day."

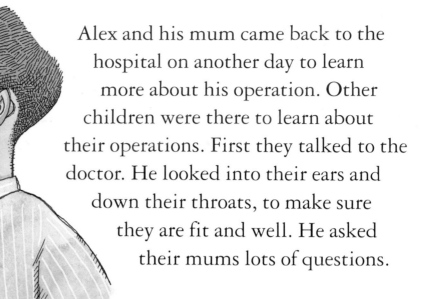

Alex and his mum came back to the hospital on another day to learn more about his operation. Other children were there to learn about their operations. First they talked to the doctor. He looked into their ears and down their throats, to make sure they are fit and well. He asked their mums lots of questions.

Mags, the play specialist, showed Alex how to take his mum's temperature in her ear, then he took his own temperature. The machine beeped and showed his temperature on the screen.

Kate is going to have her tonsils out, to stop her from getting very sore throats and feeling sick and ill. She plays with the blood pressure machine. She kept her arm very still while the strap pumped up and squeezed her arm tight, then went down again. It measures how well the blood pumps round her body.

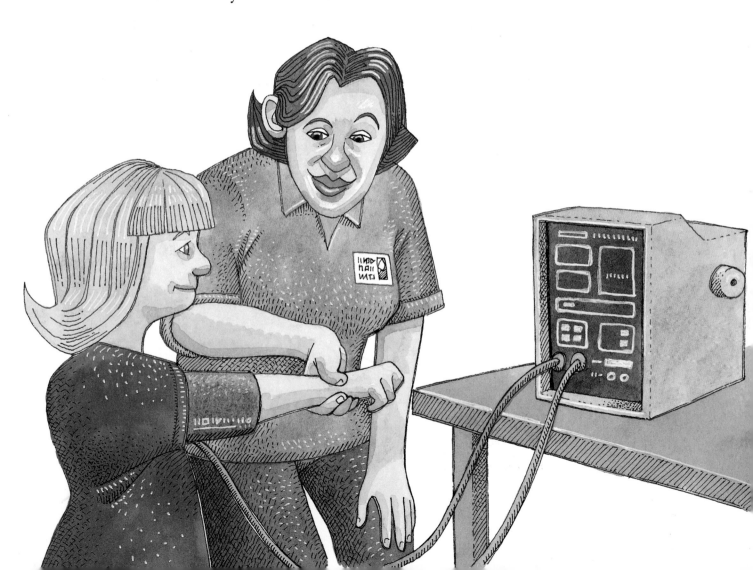

Mags shows Peter the machine which measures your heart beat and the amount of oxygen in the blood. It's a spongy peg that fits on his finger. It beeps when the numbers come up on the screen.

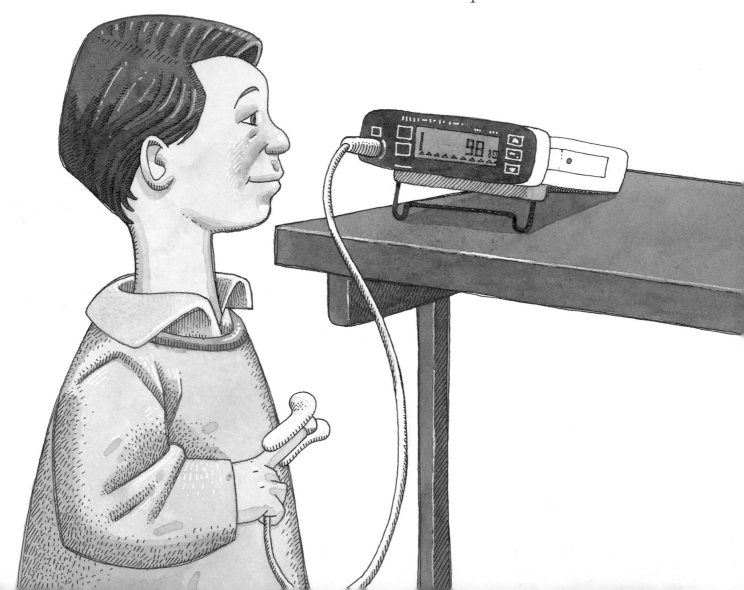

In between playing with the machines, they watch a video about having an operation.

Julia the nurse wants to know more about all the children. She tells Kate not to have breakfast on the day she comes in for her operation, "You might feel sick after the operation, so it's better to have an empty tummy."

What's your favourite food?

What's your favourite drink?

What's your favourite game?

Where do you go to school?

Mags and Julia then take the children down to see where they will sleep when they come into hospital. On the ward, there is also a playroom and a room where mums and dads can be quiet. It's a warm day so some of the children are playing outside. Kate thinks it looks fun and she almost looks forward to coming into hospital.

Sam shows them his name bands. He has one on his wrist and one round his ankle. His teddy wears a name band too, so he won't get lost. Sam says that when he is given medicine the nurse always checks his name and now he knows his number off by heart.

The nurse squirts the medicine into his mouth, it doesn't taste too bad, but he has a nice drink to follow.

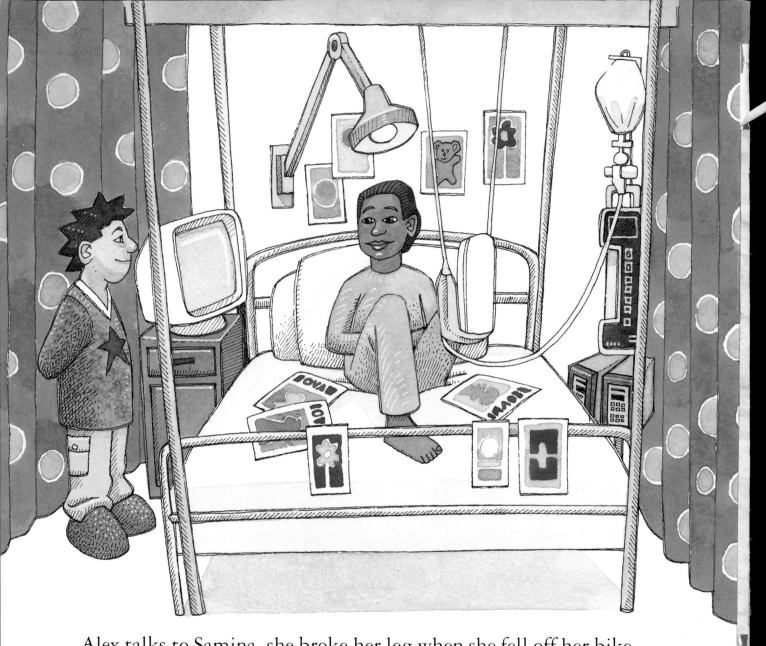

Alex talks to Samina, she broke her leg when she fell off her bike.
She's a bit bored with being in bed, even though she has her own
TV, and she can watch videos. Mum and dad take it in turns to
sleep the night with her. She tells Alex about her x-ray.

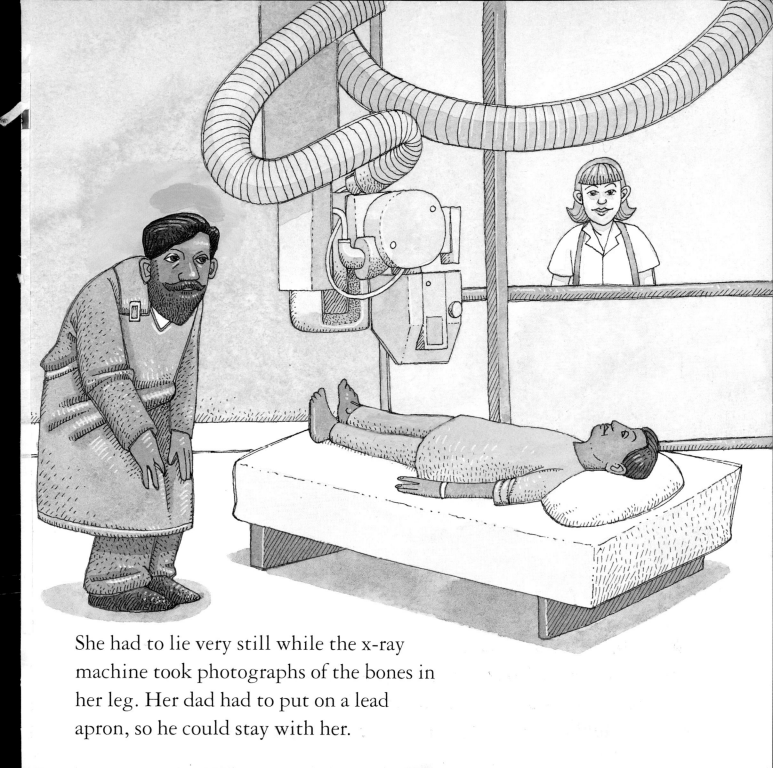

She had to lie very still while the x-ray
machine took photographs of the bones in
her leg. Her dad had to put on a lead
apron, so he could stay with her.

Oliver is catching up on his school work. The teacher gives the children lessons each morning. Oliver has lost all his hair. He explains that he had cancer. He was given very strong medicine to kill the cancer cells and the medicine made his hair fall out. It also made him feel sick. He's much better now and soon he'll be going home. His hair will soon start to grow back again.

Ben came to hospital in an ambulance. He had a very bad pain in his tummy. He has had an operation to make him better. He felt quite sore for a bit and didn't want to get out of bed. When he wanted to go to the toilet the nurse brought him a special potty.

Anne has got to have a blood test. Mags the play specialist goes into the treatment room with her. She lets Anne blow bubbles while the lady pricks her finger and squeezes out a few drops of blood. Anne says "ouch", but she agrees it didn't hurt much.

Kate and Alex come in to hospital on the same day. They are given beds in the same room, so they can keep each other company. Kate has brought her nightclothes, wash bag and slippers and they both have their teddies. Kate and her mum put their clothes in the locker by her bed. Her mum's bed can be pulled down from the cupboard beside Kate's bed.

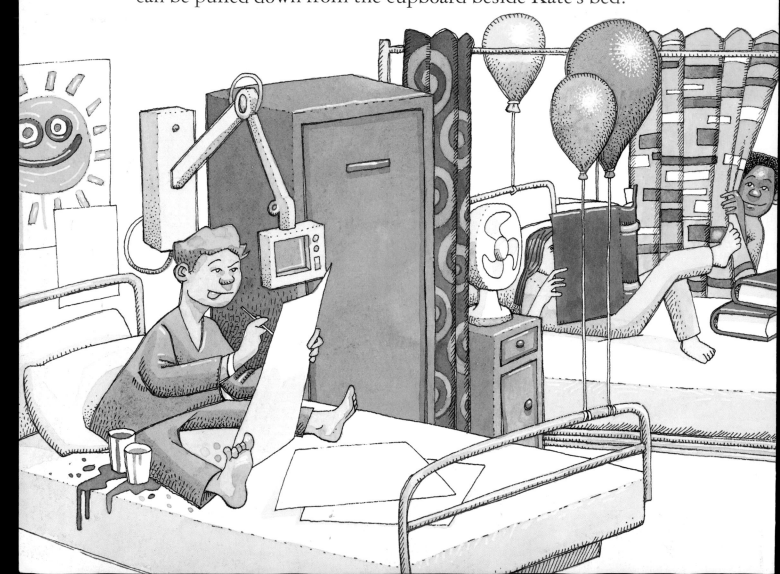

The nurse puts on their name bands. Kate and Alex are weighed and have their blood pressure and temperatures taken. Then they go off to the playroom to find Mags. Their mums can go to the parent's room to have coffee.

Alex has gone to have his operation. A doctor called an anaesthetist comes to talk to Kate and her mum. Kate thinks she's wearing her pyjamas. She will give Kate the medicine, called anaesthetic which will make her sleep during the operation.

The nurse puts some cream on the backs of Kate's hands. She calls it magic cream, because it will make a little numb patch on the back of her hands, so she won't feel the injection of anaesthetic. Kate's mum helps her change into her gown for the operation.

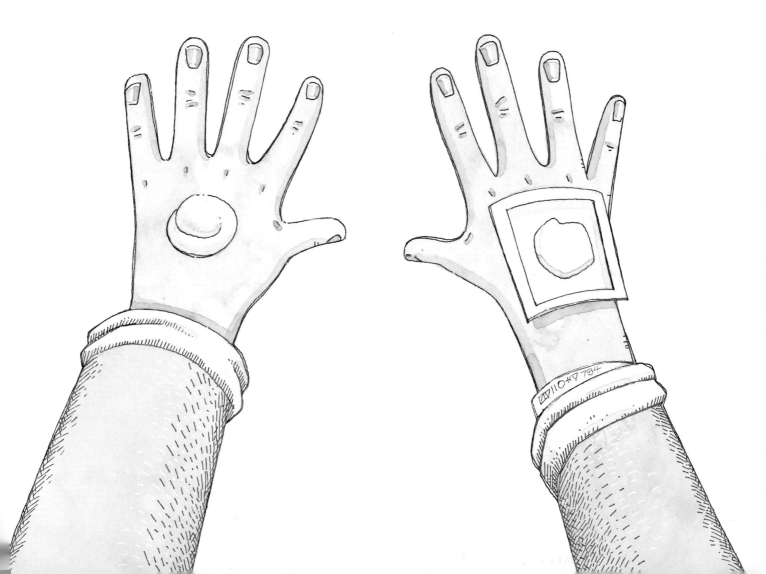

Kate and her mum walk down to the operating
theatre, and someone pushes her bed behind her.

The anaesthetist lifts her up on to the bed. Kate feels a slight push as he puts a tiny tube into the back of her hand. Kate thinks 'the cream is magic, it didn't hurt at all.' The anaesthetist injects the anaesthetic through the tube into her hand. Her mum gives her a kiss, and she's fast asleep.

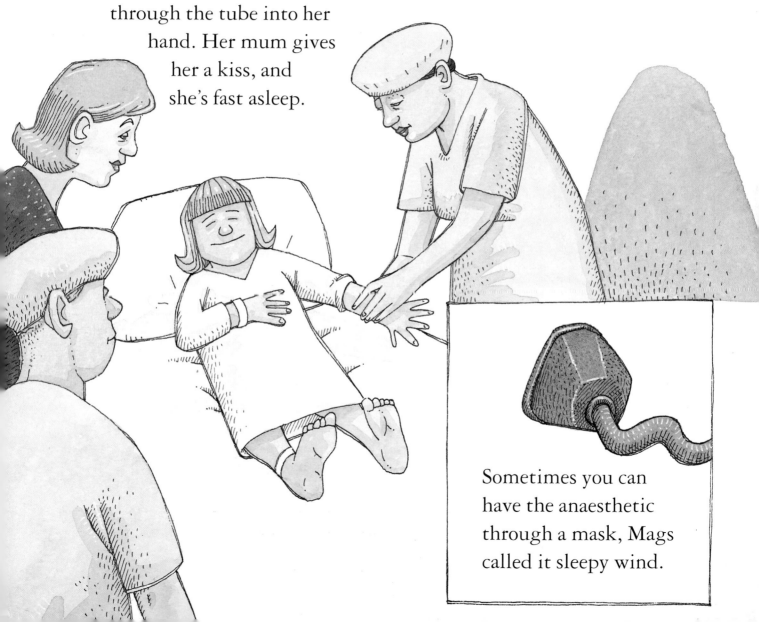

Sometimes you can have the anaesthetic through a mask, Mags called it sleepy wind.

It seems no time at all before she is waking up. The nurse takes the oxygen mask off her face. She feels a bit dizzy, but mum is there to hold her hand, and to tell her it's all over. Later she is pushed back to the ward in her bed.

Alex comes to say goodbye, he has had
his operation too, and he can go home.

The next morning Kate is given some medicine to make her throat feel less sore. It's no sorer than it used to be when she had tonsillitis and this time it's going to get better for good. She manages to eat some cornflakes and toast for breakfast. The doctor says she can go home. She says goodbye to all her new friends.

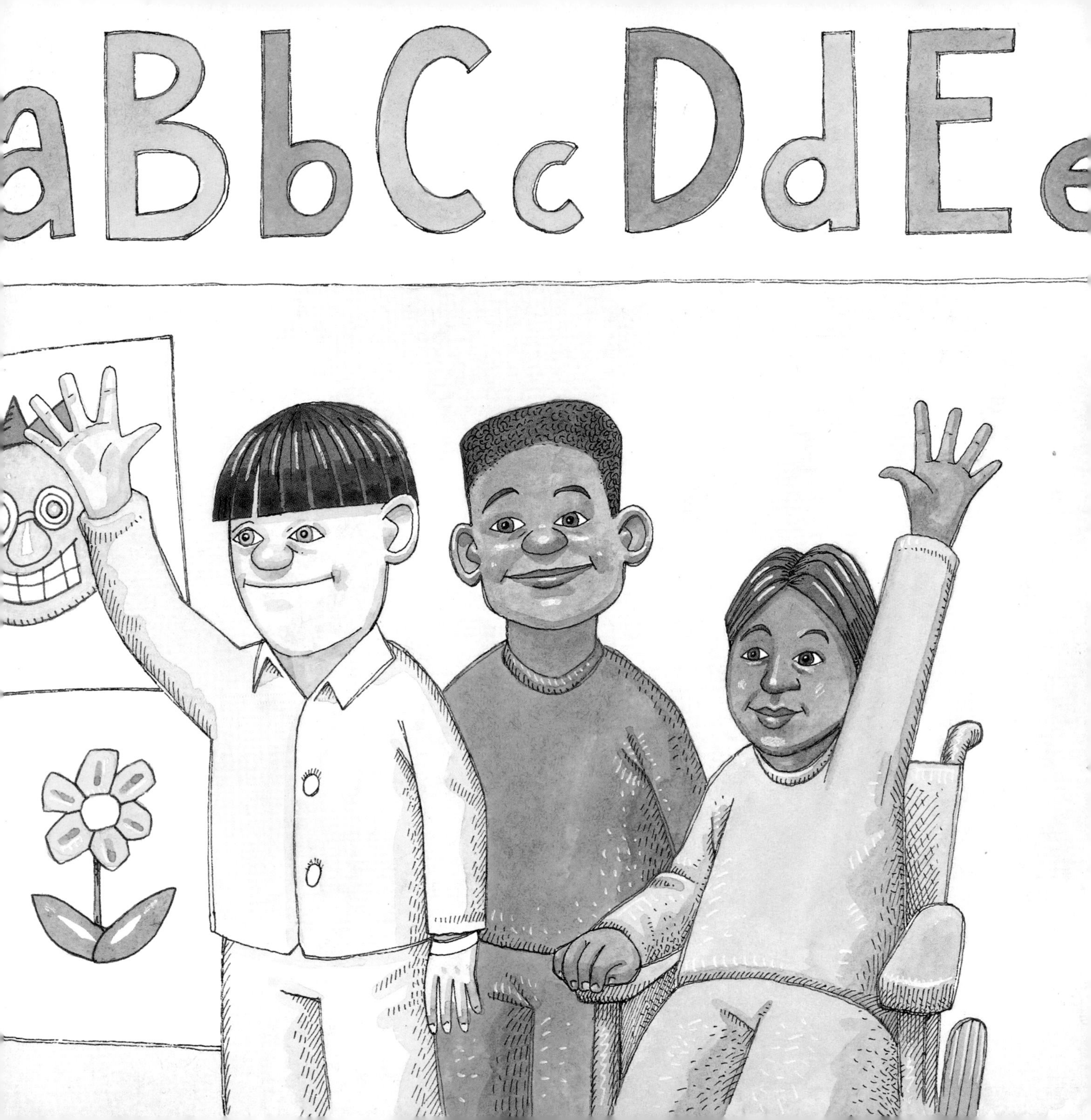
aBbCcDdEe

Children can be worried about coming to hospital for a number of reasons; this is often brought about by the fear of the unknown.

Althea's book explains some of the more common sights and procedures children may encounter on a visit to hospital.

In a positive and reassuring manner, it can be used as preparation for a planned hospital admission, and gives the child the opportunity to discuss and ask questions.

Even when a hospital admission is not an issue, this informative book would be a useful addition to any child's book collection, as it provides both parent and child with an insight in to what takes place on a children's ward.

Jackie McClelland
Hospital Play Co-ordinator,
Addenbrooke's N.H.S. Trust